Just what is it about veteran and vintage cars that makes us stop and look; that exerts such fascination for people of all ages? By comparison with today's vehicles they are invariably temperamental, noisy, unreliable, slow, complex and certainly some of them are cold and total strangers to weatherproofing in any form. And yet care and attention is lavished on them out of all proportion to their usefulness as actual conveyances. Indeed, in many cases their use as conveyances is hardly considered except for the occasional rally organised by and for their owners and admirers.

One of the reasons for their popularity is obviously their curiosity value. Their monetary value would seem another obvious attraction. Like any antiques, these old vehicles tend to increase in value as they become scarcer. Yet most owners of, or enthusiasts for, these particular treasures would deny that their monetary worth is a prime consideration, if it is considered at all.

To the student of technology they are certainly a source of endless fascination. Almost all vehicles we now call veteran or vintage embody some innovatory technology, perhaps even a breakthrough, and the way ignition, cooling, carburation, gearboxes, suspension and so on developed is there to see.

Nostalgia for its own sake notwithstanding, they are a tangible link with the past; a past that is recent enough for us to have some knowledge of, and a working link at that! These vehicles, for the most part, still work, and that is tribute indeed to the men who designed and built them and to the present owners who have, in many cases, rescued them from a seemingly irreparable state and lovingly restored them.

Today's cars can, by definition, eventually become veteran and vintage; all it takes is time. But they can never be true originals, precursers of an era, hand-built and idiosyncratic according to their designers' and builders' whim – and maybe that is a large part of the charm of these survivors from another era.

Previous page: the four-cylinder "Unic" 12/14 hp model was one of the most successful of the company's products. It achieved fame as a London taxi and like its modern-day counterpart it boasted reliability and small turning circle. *Facing page:* the Gladiator of 1896 was powered by a 6 hp twin-cylinder engine. *This page clockwise from above:* the 1896 Leon Bollée Tricar, the 4 hp "Orient Express" of 1898, the 6 CV La Croix de la Ville of 1898 and the 1895 Knight.

The 1903 Argyll 10/12 *facing page* was one of the first cars to feature gate change. *Above:* the Beeston Quad of 1899 carried its passenger forward of the saddle-seated driver. *Top right:* it was with machines such as this 30 hp of 1900 that Napier became justifiably famous. *Right:* a 6 hp Daimler of 1900. *Below:* the 10 hp Albion of 1900 was primitive, even by the standards of the day.

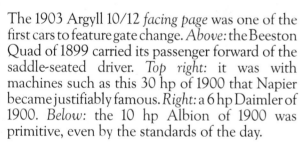

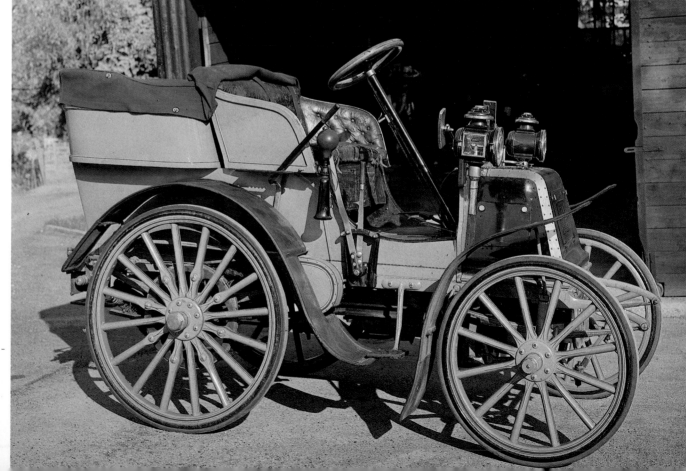

Whilst some early models achieved a surprising degree of sophistication, others retained the appearance of horseless-carriages. *Clockwise from above:* a Baby Peugeot of 1902, a 1901 8 hp Durkopp, the 1899 Cannstatt Daimler, a 1900 5 hp Clément-Panhard. *Facing page:* the 6 hp Humberette of 1903.

*Above:* a 1903 Gladiator. Originally a bicycle manufacturer, this French firm began making cars in 1896. *Right:* the American built Conrad car of 1902 used a 12 hp 2 cylinder two-stroke engine. *Below:* a 1903 8 hp De Dion-Bouton. *Bottom right:* a 15 hp 2 cylinder Stevens Duryea. *Facing page:* a magnificent 7/9 Vauxhall of 1904.

A quartet of French-made cars: the 1903 9 hp Gladiator *top left*, a De Dion-Bouton 8 hp of 1902 *above*, a Georges Richard model of 1903 *below* and a two-seater De Dion-Bouton 6 hp of 1903 *bottom left*. *Facing page:* the powerful 9.5 litre 70 hp Mercedes of 1904.

*Clockwise from above:* a 1904 De Dietrich, a 1904 Sunbeam, a 1909 Humber and an American-made White of 1903. *Facing page:* a 1904 Humberette.

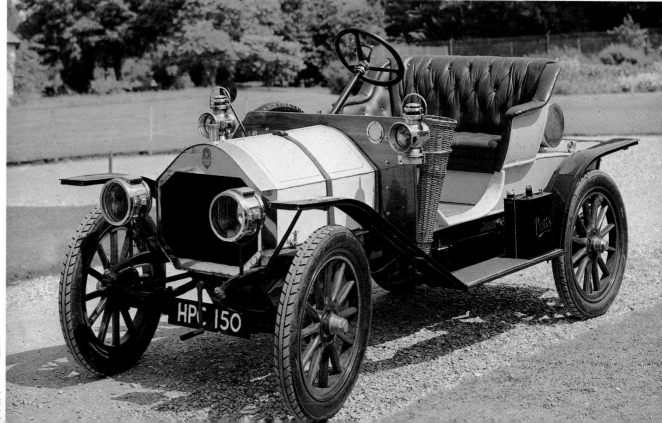

The 6 cylinder 9.5 litre engine of the 1904 Mercedes *above* was one of Maybach's last designs for the company. *Top right:* the 8 hp Stanley Steam Car of 1904 was surprisingly nimble, outperforming many contemporary petrol-driven machines. *Right:* a 1903 Panhard Levassor Phaeton with side chain final drive. *Below:* Oldsmobile had the distinction of making the world's first mass-produced car; pictured is the 7 hp model of 1904. *Facing page:* a 1906 20 hp Buick.

*Above:* a two-seater De Dion-Bouton 6 hp of 1904. *Right:* a 1906 Lion-Peugeot single-cylinder tourer. *Below:* a 1906 20/30 hp Renault limousine. *Bottom right:* a 1906 Cadillac. *Facing page:* a 4 cylinder 16/20 hp car from the short-lived firm of Prosper-Lambert.

One of only three such cars ever to be built, the 4 cylinder 5.8 litre Hutton Napier *left* won the 1908 Tourist Trophy. *Above:* the 1908 Sizaire Naudin roadster, powered by a single-cylinder engine, was capable of a top speed in excess of 80 km/h. *Bottom left:* The De Dion company boasted a particularly wide and complex model range. Pictured is a 4.5 hp variant. *Below:* a 1908 Lanchester. *Facing page:* a splendid Renault 20/30 hp landaulette of 1907.

*Above:* a 17hp 1910 De Dion-Bouton. *Top right:* a 1911 7 hp Swift and *below:* a 4 cylinder American-made Traveler of the same year. Considered one of the finest cars of the time was the 1908 35 hp Delaunay Belleville *right. Facing page:* a Garrard Speke Sociable of 1911.

Top left: a 1912 Leon Bollée with somewhat unconventional lines. Below left: the 1912 12 hp Rover tourer. Above: typically French in appearance, this 1911 Renault was powered by a 7 hp version of the popular 2 cylinder engine. The Hispano-Suiza tourer of 1912 below, sometimes referred to as the Alfonso XIII, had a pair-cast 4 cylinder T-head engine. Facing page: the single-cylinder C.I.D. Baby of 1912.

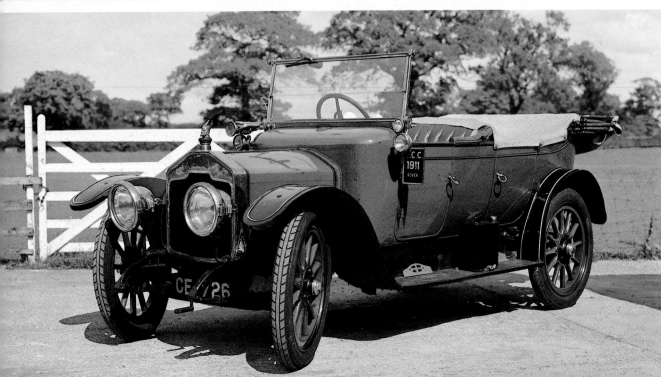

The 3 litre Peugeot racer of 1913 *below* appears remarkably modern when compared with the Renault *right* of the same year. The Stellite of 1914 *top right* was an economy 4 cylinder car made by a subsidiary of the Wolseley company. *Above:* an 8 hp 1908 Rover. *Facing page:* the Humberette, shown here in 1913 form, was a lightweight alternative to the larger Humber.

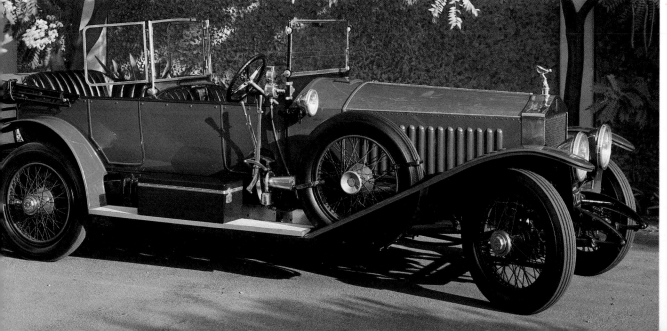

The 7 hp Swift of 1913 *facing page* was a cyclecar in the truest sense. *Left*: the Rolls-Royce Silver Ghost 40/50 hp, equipped with rear Auster screen. *Above*: a 12 hp Opel tourer from 1914. *Top left*: like most other makes, Napier cars appeared in a number of different guises. Illustrated is a commercial body mounted on a 1914 15 hp chassis. *Below*: a 1914 Darracq 12/16 hp two-seater.

Over 15 million units of the immortal Ford Model T were made between 1908 and 1927. Shown *below* is a 1915 17 hp version and *bottom right* a somewhat different 1914 example. Equipped with tiller steering, the 1908 Lanchester *above* contrasts sharply with the 1913 tourer of the same make *facing page*. *Top left*: a 1914 20 hp Sunbeam.

The touring Premier of 1919 *above* used an advanced 6 cylinder aluminium engine of 4.8 litres. *Top right:* the two-seater Perry cyclecar of 1914. Models of the Cadillac such as pictured *below* supported the maker's claim to be the 'Standard of the world.' *Bottom right:* the 1914 4.5 litre Mercedes racer. *Facing page:* the 1914 Nimble Nine was Enfield's version of the Alladay Midget.

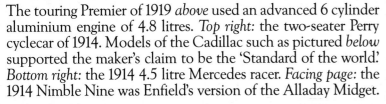

Distinguished by its 'built-in' lights, the 1915 model 48 Pierce Arrow *facing page* was powered by an 8.5 litre 6 cylinder engine. Also relying on the straight-six type layout was the 1912 Rolls-Royce Silver Ghost, shown *below* with sporting bodywork, while Austin's more successful models such as the 1914 example *left* used the well-tried 4 cylinder unit. *Bottom left*: one of three Ballot racers built for the 1919 Indianapolis 500. Also Ballot-designed was the engine of the 1915 Alba *above*.

The typical 'bull-nose' design of the Morris cars makes them instantly recognisable. Pictured *above* is the popular 12 hp Cowley of 1924. Also distinguished by their round radiator and bonnet shape were the highly acclaimed Delaunay Bellevilles. Shown *right* is a 1924 tourer. The 1924 Humpmobile *top right* marked the firm's entry into 6 cylinder car production. *Facing page*: a 14 hp 4 cylinder Donnet Zedel tourer.

*Above:* a 1923 12.8 hp Sunbeam. *Left:* the long-lived 10 hp tourer was one of Singer's most successful models. *Bottom left:* a 1922 two-seater version of the famed Morris Cowley. The Rolland Pilain racer of 1923 *below* boasted a top speed of 180 km/h. *Facing page:* the 4.3 litre V-8 Wills Sainte Claire A-68 from 1922.

Facing page: a 1923 Ford Model T. Above: the 1926 21 hp Jewett was basically a rebodied 6 cylinder Paige. Below: an 11 hp Zedel tourer of 1923. Top right: king of the supreme Bugattis; the 12.7 litre type 41 'Royale,' of which only 6 were ever built. Right: unconventional but fast, the 1926 three-wheel Morgan.

B·28636

PIZ 530

*Above:* a 1921 Hillman. *Facing page:* the 15.9 hp Star of 1920. *Below:* the 3 litre Bentley 'Speed Model' of 1926. *Left:* a 1928 4.5 litre tourer.

YP 1048

XV 9156

A product of the firm's French factory, the Hispano-Suiza "Boulogne" of 1928 *top left* had a top speed of up to 110 mph. Rather more sedate was the 1926 18 hp Armstrong Siddley *bottom left*. *Above:* a 1928 1.5 litre Lea Francis doctor's coupé. *Below:* an Ours double phaeton. *Facing page:* the fast 8 cylinder Rolland Pilain of 1923.

Bottom left: a 4 cylinder supercharged Bugatti type 40 coupé. *Above:* the formidable straight-eight Stutz of 1929. *Below:* a 1928 model 17 hp 6 cylinder Peugeot. *Left:* a 4 cylinder 8 hp Opel of 1928. *Facing page:* an impressive 6 cylinder Lorraine Dietrich tourer of 1925.

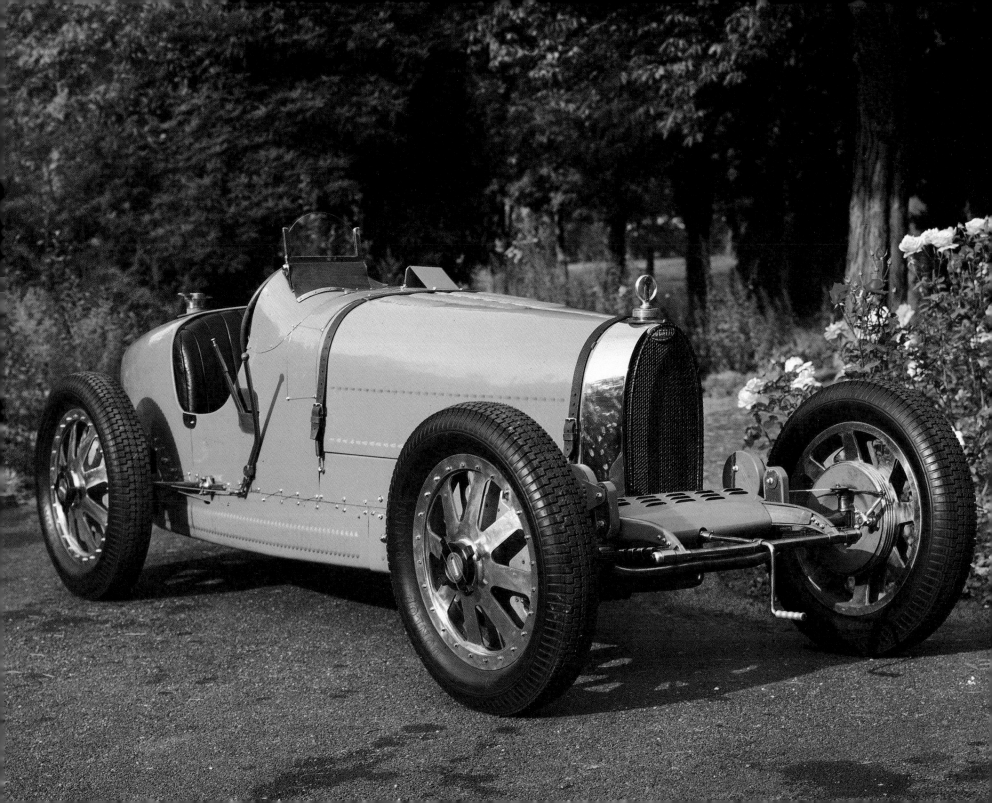

The horseshoe-shaped radiators of the invincible Bugattis were a common sight on the starting grid at most major race meetings. Shown *facing page* is the elegant 1926 2.3 litre type 35 Targa. Powered by a straight-8, the Delage racer *right* of 1927 was to achieve considerable success in competition. At the top of the luxury sports car market, however, were such cars as the 6 cylinder Hispano-Suiza 'Boulogne' *above* and the superb Bentley Speed-Six *bottom right* of 1929. Sunbeam, with such models as the 3 litre 6 cylinder of 1929 *far right*, also had a reputation for speed. Modest by comparison, the Riley Nine *below* was nevertheless competitive in its class. *Overleaf*: the fast Vauxhall 30/98 OE tourer of 1927.

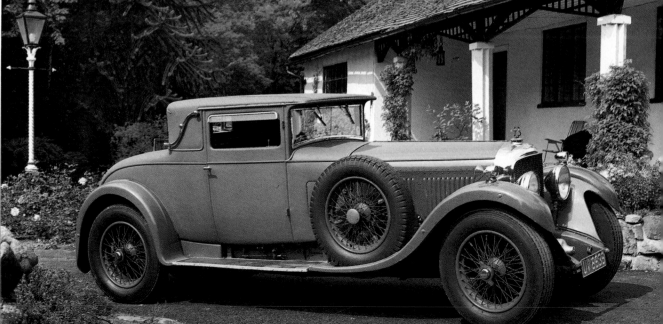

Dep. Leg. B. 21.931/83

# Collectors Series
## 1948 MG-TC

In the years immediately preceding World War II, a few automobile designs reached their classic zenith, most notably the Cadillac and the MG. Combining the reckless spirit of the motorcycle—with its spoked wheels and midget body, and the proletarian popularity of the buggy—with its running boards and folding top, the MG (Morris Garage Company) TC achieved what many feel is the essence of "everyman's sports car." The TC model was almost identical to the TB, whose production was interrupted by the war. Because demand in the post-war period was far ahead of supply (especially for the sports car) and because tooling money was not available until the early 50's for a replacement model, this classic design was allowed to continue unaltered through 1949, and thus was to become one of the most sought-after two-seaters in the history of British automobiles. Like the ivy league cap, the briar pipe and the tweed sports jacket, this ragtop roadster was a casual, affordable and understated expression of self-indulgence and snobbery in the British tradition.

Although its 0-60 mph acceleration could hardly be described as earth-shattering (actually slower than most modern non-turbo diesels), the experience of driving this 1,300 pound vehicle whose spoke wheels could still grip the road at 80 miles per hour like a desperate feline could still be described as exhilarating. Detroit is only now beginning to appreciate the handling characteristics achieved in these early precursors of today's small performance cars.

True aficionados were appalled by MG's move toward more "modern" body styling, "gutsier" performance and "unnecessary" refinements such as independent front suspension and disc wheels in the TD series, beginning in 1950. The hardy little roadster affectionately rendered here literally brought the automobile road racing experience within the means of the average American car enthusiast in the late 1940's and nurtured the philosophy and camaraderie which eventually blossomed into today's Sports Car Club of America.

## About the Artist:

William Kuhlman has been a professional illustrator and graphic designer for over 30 years. Bill often works in watercolor, as in this series of classic car illustrations especially commissioned by Opinion Survey Center, Inc. Mr. Kuhlman's love of fine automobiles parallels his enthusiasm for his craft. His original work, as expertly reproduced here, reflects not only his painstaking attention to detail, but also his undying appreciation of the personality of the automobiles—an appreciation nurtured through years of study and experience. Bill's "preoccupation" with engines and wheels in many of his illustrations is also the driving force in his hobby— collecting and restoring vintage motorcycles. Mr. Kuhlman's art has graced many calendars and advertisements throughout his career. He currently maintains a studio in Perrysburg, Ohio.

A special, three-color process using black, brown and opaque white ink on Hopper Feltweave natural cover stock was used to authentically reproduce the subtle effects of the watercolors in these illustrations.

# Collectors Series
## 1948 MG-TC

In the years immediately preceding World War II, a few automobile designs reached their classic zenith, most notably the Cadillac and the MG. Combining the reckless spirit of the motorcycle—with its spoked wheels and midget body, and the proletarian popularity of the buggy—with its running boards and folding top, the MG (Morris Garage Company) TC achieved what many feel is the essence of "everyman's sports car." The TC model was almost identical to the TB, whose production was interrupted by the war. Because demand in the post-war period was far ahead of supply (especially for the sports car) and because tooling money was not available until the early 50's for a replacement model, this classic design was allowed to continue unaltered through 1949, and thus was to become one of the most sought-after two-seaters in the history of British automobiles. Like the ivy league cap, the briar pipe and the tweed sports jacket, this ragtop roadster was a casual, affordable and under-stated expression of self-indulgence and snobbery in the British tradition.

Although its 0-60 mph acceleration could hardly be described as earth-shattering (actually slower than most modern non-turbo diesels), the experience of driving this 1,300 pound vehicle whose spoke wheels could still grip the road at 80 miles per hour like a desperate feline could still be described as exhilarating. Detroit is only now beginning to appreciate the handling characteristics achieved in these early precursors of today's small performance cars.

True aficionados were appalled by MG's move toward more "modern" body styling, "gutsier" performance and "unnecessary" refinements such as independent front suspension and disc wheels in the TD series, beginning in 1950. The hardy little roadster affectionately rendered here literally brought the automobile road racing experience within the means of the average American car enthusiast in the late 1940's and nurtured the philosophy and camaraderie which eventually blossomed into today's Sports Car Club of America.

### About the Artist:

William Kuhlman has been a professional illustrator and graphic designer for over 30 years. Bill often works in watercolor, as in this series of classic car illustrations especially commissioned by Opinion Survey Center, Inc. Mr. Kuhlman's love of fine automobiles parallels his enthusiasm for his craft. His original work, as expertly reproduced here, reflects not only his painstaking attention to detail, but also his undying appreciation of the personality of the automobiles—an appreciation nurtured through years of study and experience. Bill's "preoccupation" with engines and wheels in many of his illustrations is also the driving force in his hobby—collecting and restoring vintage motorcycles. Mr. Kuhlman's art has graced many calendars and advertisements throughout his career. He currently maintains a studio in Perrysburg, Ohio.